SELF-MANAGEMENT

Self-management can help you to be more organized at home, at work, and at school.

THE LEARNING-A-LIVING LIBRARY

High Performance Through
SELF-
MANAGEMENT

Peggy Santamaria

THE ROSEN PUBLISHING GROUP, INC.
NEW YORK

Published in 1996 by The Rosen Publishing Group, Inc.
29 East 21st Street, New York, NY 10010

First Edition

Printed in the United States of America

Library of Congress Cataloging-in-Publication Data

Santamaria, Peggy.
    High performance through self-management / Peggy Santamaria.
      p. cm. — (The learning-a-living library)
    Includes bibliographical references and index.
    Summary: Specific tips on acquiring self-management skills applicable to school and work activities.
    ISBN 0-8239-2208-1
    1. Teenagers—Time management—Juvenile literature. 2. Time management—Juvenile literature. 3. Self-management (Psychology) for teenagers—Juvenile literature. [1. Time management. 2. Life skills.] I. Title. II. Series.
BF637.T5S36 1996
640'.43'0835—dc20   95-38830
                                        CIP
                                        AC

Contents

Learning self-management techniques now can help to prepare you for future success.

Overview of SELF-MANAGEMENT

MOST STUDENTS HAVE BEEN IN A CLASSROOM AT one time or another and asked themselves, "Why do I need to learn this stuff? How will I ever use this in my life?" Sometimes it is difficult to see how what you are learning could be useful to you. One frustrated young woman once pleaded, "Please don't teach me anything new. I already know more than I understand."

In the following chapters, you'll find some ideas that you can understand and use. These ideas are about you. They are ideas that you can use right now. They can help you accomplish what you need to in school and at work. They can help you get what you want in the future. These ideas can help you achieve the things that are important to you.

You will be looking at ideas for *self-management*. What does that mean? Self-management is nothing more than directing yourself.

Through self-management, you can complete work that is assigned to you. You can identify what is most important to do first. You can schedule your time to do the things you need and want to do. You can set your own goals. Self-management offers you the tools to reach *high performance levels.*

The book introduces people who use self-management in school, on the job, in activities, and in planning for the future. The skills discussed are those that employers are looking for in today's competitive workplace. They are skills that will give you an edge by making you more productive.

Learning the principles of self-management gives you the opportunity to take greater control of your own life. Making these ideas part of your own life can be well worth the time you spend learning them.

Questions to Ask Yourself

Self-management can help you to achieve your goals for the future. 1) Where would you like to be, and what would you like to be doing, in five years? In ten years? 2) Which of your daily tasks would you like to accomplish more efficiently? 3) Do you feel that you could be more productive?

Basic Steps for Self-Management

IF TAKING CHARGE OF YOUR LIFE SOUNDS GOOD TO you, take a look at the following list of steps that can help you do so:

1. Take responsibility.
2. Set goals.
3. Schedule your time.
4. Evaluate your progress.

Think about each of these steps, and be sure you understand what each one means. These will be your building blocks for developing your self-management techniques.

Step 1: Take responsibility

When children are very young, they begin letting their parents know that they want to make their own decisions. They don't want to be told when to go to bed or when to do homework. Children want to be independent and responsible.

The difficult part about being responsible is that

One of the basic steps in self-management is to set a goal. Your long-term goal may be to buy a car, for example.

if anything goes wrong, there is no one to blame but yourself. It is always easier if someone else has caused you to fail. You can get mad at that person, or tell everyone that it is not your fault. Most people would rather say they were late for work because the bus broke down than because they overslept.

In self-management, you are responsible for yourself. You are able to take initiative. This means you have the ability to take the first step and begin working toward a goal. When you succeed, you can feel very proud. Taking responsibility is challenging.

Step 2: Setting goals

Everyone knows what a goal is. It is something you want to reach, or win, or achieve. Most goals are not easy to reach. You work for them and move toward them step by step. Often, you set a goal because of a problem or a need. For instance, you have no transportation, so you set a goal of buying a car.

A goal is different from a wish because once you have set your goal, you also begin planning the steps you will take to reach that goal. You begin to make it a reality, not just a dream. If your goal is to buy a car, you may choose steps like:

- getting a job
- saving money
- finding a reliable car to buy.

These steps that you choose to help you reach your goal are called *objectives*. Objectives are like small goals that you must reach in order to get to the big goal.

Step 3: Scheduling your time

Besides setting your goal and planning your objectives, you also need to set aside the time to meet those objectives and reach that goal. You need to be realistic in scheduling your time. You wouldn't schedule fifteen minutes on a Saturday night for a movie that you have been waiting to see; that would not even give you enough time to buy popcorn. Scheduling the time to follow through on your plans is a big part of achieving what you want.

Step 4: Evaluating your progress

Evaluating your progress means checking to see how you are doing about carrying out your plans. You need to be honest with yourself when doing this. You need to ask yourself whether you are achieving what you said you would and whether you are on schedule.

When you begin to evaluate, you may find that things are not working out as you had planned. This is nothing to worry about. It is an opportunity to try another plan or make a new schedule. This step is also called self-evaluation because you are evaluating yourself. No one wants you to succeed as much as you do, and you have the power to make that happen.

Applying These Steps

If you begin to use these steps in your everyday life, you will find that your ability to achieve your goals is improving. It is often a challenge to take responsibility, set goals, schedule your time, and evaluate your progress. However, these are powerful tools used effectively by many people. Used in combination, they will help you to achieve high performance through self-management, too.

Questions to Ask Yourself

The basic steps of self-management are: take responsibility, set goals, schedule your time, and evaluate your progress. 1) What is the difference between a wish and a goal? 2) What is an objective? Why are objectives important? 3) Do you have a goal that you would like to achieve?

Schedules, calendars, and notepads can help you get organized.

Self-Management at School

NOW THAT YOU HAVE READ THE BASIC CONCEPTS of self-management, let's look at how these ideas are put into practice by someone at school.

Michael has a problem. His grade in English has dropped, and he wants to get a better grade this term. Michael plays guitar in a band. He has an agreement with his parents that if he keeps his grades up, he can use the family car to go to band practice.

When he got his grades last marking period, he told his parents that it wasn't his fault that the English grade was low; he said it was really the teacher's fault. He said the teacher was too hard, and he didn't explain the assignments clearly enough. Michael felt that he was not responsible for what had happened. But his parents remained firm, saying that if he wanted to continue to use the car for band practice, he would have to bring up the grade.

Michael moped around for a while, telling his friends that his parents weren't fair and that his teacher wasn't fair. He said that no one ever gave him a break. He blamed everyone except himself for his situation.

After a few days, however, Michael decided that he needed to find a way to change it. He wanted to be able to go to practice with his friends in the band. He enjoyed playing his guitar and really had fun playing with the group.

Learning About Responsibility

Michael started thinking about what he could do. First, he thought maybe he would just ask the teacher to raise the grade. But right away he knew that was a silly idea. Michael had to do something himself.

Thinking it over, he began to realize that it really had not been the teacher's fault that his grade went down. Michael had not bothered to do a few of his assignments. He turned some in late even though the teacher had said that following the schedule was an important part of the assignment. He could see now that he had not acted responsibly.

The next day in English class the teacher announced a research paper that would be a big part of the grade for the period. He told the class that the purpose of the assignment was to see if the students could organize their time and information and follow instructions. He wanted the class to learn to

You'll find that sitting around just doesn't get you where you want to go.

schedule work in order to accomplish an assignment. Michael listened very carefully. This could be his chance. He was taking his first steps in learning to be responsible for his own work.

Taking Action

Michael began to write down what the teacher was saying. He knew that if he was going to get it right this time, he would need to pay attention. The teacher said that the paper could be about any event in American history. He wanted the students to choose their topics, get books from the library for research, write an outline, complete a rough draft of the paper, and present a final version of the paper about the event. He gave them a schedule to follow:

1. By next Friday, write and turn in a statement of the event in history to be researched, and a list of three books to be used for research about the event.
2. By the following Friday, hand in an outline for the paper.
3. By the third Friday, hand in a rough draft of the paper.
4. By the fourth Friday, hand in the completed paper.

The teacher was very specific about what the students were to do and when they were to do it. Michael made sure to write everything down carefully.

Michael had stopped blaming the teacher for his low grade. He realized that, previously, he had not followed instructions. He also saw that he could now choose to act differently. Michael was learning about responsibility.

Learning to Set Goals

Michael walked home slowly after school that day. He had a lot to think about. It wasn't enough just to wish his English grade would get better; he was going to have to do something to make that happen.

Take the time to think about your goals and what you need to do to accomplish them.

He would get his research paper done on time.
That would be his goal.

Michael's father had often spoken to him about
setting goals in order to be successful and achieve
things in life. Michael decided to set this goal and
act responsibly to achieve it. But he wondered how
he would go about it. He needed a plan of action.

Later at home, Michael read over his notes from
class. He saw that completing each of the assigned
steps in the project was an objective to be met.
These were four little goals he would need to accomplish in order to achieve his big goal.

Michael was beginning to act rather than to wish.

To maintain the progress of a plan, you will need to complete one task before going on to the next one.

He was learning to set a goal and choose the objectives to help him reach that goal.

Learning to Schedule

That night, Michael made notes on the calendar in his room. He marked the dates when each part of the assignment was due. As he looked at the calendar, he realized that he would also need to schedule the time needed to do the work required for each step of the project.

Step 1, choosing a topic, wouldn't be too difficult. He was in an American history class. He would choose something he was studying in class. He would choose a topic that night after he finished his homework.

However, getting a list of library books would take a little more thought. He would need to plan a trip to the library in time to find the books he would need. He decided to go to the library on Saturday. That would give him plenty of time in case he had trouble finding what he needed.

Step 2, compiling an outline, would be the hardest part for him. He might need some help on that. So he marked three days in the week before the outline was due. That would give him time to work on the outline and to ask his teacher any questions he might have about it. He would do this work right after school.

Step 3, writing a rough draft, would help Michael figure out the best way to set up his paper. He knew that feedback on the rough draft from his teacher would make the final paper better, so he planned to put a lot of time into making it a good presentation of his material. He decided to work on it each night during the week before it was due. That way, he wouldn't have to write it all at once. He recalled that one time he had needed to stay up all night before band practice to learn a song because he had put off studying it. He did not want to go through that again with his paper.

Step 4, completing the paper, seemed a long way off, but Michael knew that it would come quickly. So, Michael planned to work on revising his rough draft both the Saturday and Sunday before the paper was due. He would also save some time each night that week to work on it if necessary.

What Michael had done was schedule his time to be sure he would be able to meet each objective. If he was able to do this, he would be able to achieve his goal.

Following Through

Michael began following his schedule. He did this even on nights when he was tired and didn't feel like working. Soon he found he was able to accomplish more each evening. He could schedule time each night to practice his guitar and still get all his work done. He was learning to manage his time by scheduling, and it was helping him to be more productive.

In the third week of his project, Michael's friends asked him to join them after school. He didn't bother to think about what he had scheduled for that day. He just went along with them and had a good time.

Before going to bed that night, Michael looked at his calendar and realized that he had not worked on his outline at all, and he had planned to start it that day. This was going to be the most difficult part of the assignment for him, and he knew it would take the most time. He had lost an important day's work. He began to worry about it.

Learning Self-Evaluation

When he began working on his project, Michael had found that he was able to keep up with his schedule. He had turned in his topic a day early, and the teacher had congratulated him. But now he would need to reorganize his plan. He no longer had the three days he needed to work on his outline.

Because he had neglected to follow through responsibly, Michael knew he would need to work harder and longer each day to get his outline completed on time.

He decided that each morning he would look at his project schedule and make a note to take to school about the work he needed to do that day.

Reworking the Plan

Michael knew he would need to ask his teacher for help on the outline. He made an appointment to see him that day. He realized there would be no time to play guitar or to watch television that night if he hoped to get this assignment handed in on time.

He was able to meet his deadline with the help of his teacher and some extra hard work.

Learning from Self-Evaluation

Michael was learning about self-evaluation. He was learning that checking on his progress could result in seeing the need to change his plan and the way he was doing his work. He learned that he wanted to stick to his schedule and continue to be responsible. He had done what he needed to do to get himself back on schedule.

Getting There

Michael completed his rough draft and received excellent feedback from his teacher. Since he had worked hard on writing his rough draft, he didn't have to make many changes and was able to hand in his finished paper the day before it was due. He was very proud of himself, and he had a right to be proud. He had done what he thought he could not do. Michael had made the decision that if his grade was to go up, it would only be as a result of his taking responsibility. He did. He saw his goal, he noted the objectives, scheduled his time, and evaluated his progress. He realized that he had accomplished more than just getting his assignment done. He had learned an important lesson in managing his own life.

Michael will be able to use these basic techniques for managing himself to increase his performance in other subjects. He will find that he can achieve high performance at school through self-management.

Questions to Ask Yourself

At school, self-management skills can help you organize your schedule better. 1) What was the first step Michael took in improving his schedule? 2) Have you ever blamed somebody else for something that was your responsibility? Why does blaming somebody else not help you? 3) Why is follow-through an important element of having an effective schedule?

Self-Management at Work

IN THE PREVIOUS CHAPTER, WE FOLLOWED Michael as he learned to take responsibility for his own work. He found that he had the tools to accomplish his goal of getting his work done. In this chapter you will see that you can use the same ideas at work that Michael used at school. Through self-management, you can increase your performance at work.

What Is the Goal?

Michael set a goal for himself and worked to achieve it. In the workplace, you may find that a goal is presented to you and you must accomplish it. Your boss may give you a project to undertake. Your responsibility is to get the job done in the time the boss gives you. To be able to accomplish a goal at work, it is necessary to understand exactly what is expected of you. You must get the big picture. What does the boss want accomplished?

Get the Information You Need

To learn about the goal you are striving for, you must listen very carefully to what you are asked to do. This is the time to ask any questions you might have. If you do not understand, ask! You need to know as many details as possible if you are to fulfill your role as an employee.

If you are given a complicated job to handle, you may need to write some notes about what is expected and when it is to be completed. As you begin your work, you may find that you have other questions. You may find that things are happening that you did not expect. This is a good time to go back to your boss for more information or for suggestions. It is better to ask a second time than to do the job wrong and have to do it over again.

If your boss isn't available or doesn't have time to speak to you, determine whether or not you can proceed anyway. For example, your boss asked you to make fifty photocopies on pink paper. The photocopier is stocked with white paper. If you can't find pink paper anywhere in the supply room, you'd need to ask someone for help. But your boss would probably be annoyed if you asked for pink paper without trying to find it yourself first.

Where Do You Fit In?

Besides learning all about the goal, you need to

know exactly what role you are to play in achieving it. Usually in a job you will be working with other people. You will be responsible for your part. If several people are working on one project, it is good to know what part of the work each person is to do. By learning about the responsibilities of others involved in the project, you can better see how you can assist each other, or just stay out of each other's way. The group can accomplish more if each person is aware of the responsibilities of the others.

Self-Management in Groups

Employers want workers who are able to act responsibly within a group. They want workers who interact well with others. Sharing responsibility in this way is familiar to anyone who has played in a band, acted in a play, or participated in a team sport. In each of these activities it is necessary to be aware of those working with you.

This type of cooperation is referred to as a group effort. For the group effort to be successful, each member must fulfill his or her individual responsibilities. Otherwise the project may not succeed, the game may be lost, the music may sound flat, or the play may be a flop.

If one person does not fulfill responsibilities within a group, another person may be unable to complete his or her share of the work. In the ex-

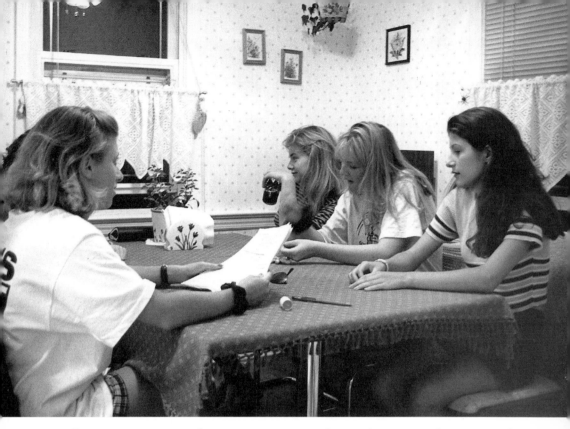

Self-management is especially important in groups, where each group member is expected to fulfill certain responsibilities.

ample of Michael, a student is responsible only for his own work. If he does not do part of it, no one but Michael is hurt by it. In the group effort it is different. The work of each person affects the work of the others and the results achieved by the group.

Planning and scheduling time in a group is also different from working alone. If you are working alone, you can vary from your schedule or change it if you wish, and no one else is affected.

When you are part of a group, scheduling can be a very important factor in success. For instance, the cast of the school play plans to get together and rehearse on Saturday afternoon. Later, half the cast members decide to rehearse on Sunday instead but fail to discuss the change with the others. The result is that neither group has a complete cast and the rehearsal is useless.

Evaluation

In a group effort, evaluation is very important. At half time, the football coach reviews progress with the team and plans strategies for the rest of the game. He or she evaluates the efforts of the players and makes changes in the team if needed. The director of a play meets with the cast after opening night and reviews the performance. The director may make changes in the play at this time if he or she sees they are needed.

Evaluation of progress, whether you are working alone or in a group, is very important. It is a time to see what is working and what needs to be changed.

On the job, it is necessary for the boss to evaluate the employees' progress. This can help the employees do a better job and be more successful because it offers an opportunity to change. But if you evaluate yourself, too, you can find your weak spots before your boss does. Get to know your own style of working. Do you work better in the morning or afternoon? Do you like deadlines, or do you prefer to work at your own pace? Knowing these things about yourself can help you pace and manage yourself.

Monique

Monique has a part-time job at a sporting goods store. She works two afternoons each week after school and on weekends. She likes her job and enjoys getting a paycheck.

The boss tells Monique and the five other employees that the store is planning a big sale in two weeks. There will be new merchandise to be priced and items in the store to be marked down for the sale. He sets a goal for the employees. They will get ready for the sale. He also points out the objectives to meet in order to a accomplish that goal: to get all sale merchandise priced and displayed.

The Group Effort on the Job

The boss divides the employees into teams to handle the jobs that need to be done. Monique is teamed up with her friend Brent to work in the stockroom opening boxes of new merchandise and making the sale tickets. The others will be rearranging the displays in the store. The boss also gives each employee a schedule of when he expects each job to be completed.

Monique makes notes of what the boss is saying.

She writes down what tasks she is to do and when she is to do them. She tacks the notes on the employee bulletin board so she can check them each day when she arrives at work. She can also check them before she goes home to be sure she has accomplished the day's tasks.

Individual Responsibility in the Group

The directions seem very clear to Monique because she listened carefully. She makes sure that she understands what she is to do. As she begins her work in the stockroom, Monique realizes that she doesn't know where she is to put the new merchandise that she prices. She asks her boss and learns how to handle this part of the job.

The following week, the boss meets with the employees to evaluate their progress. Everything seems to be on schedule. But the next day, Brent does not show up for work. He is sick. Monique reviews the remaining work to be done in the stockroom. She realizes that it will not be completed on time without the help of her partner.

Taking Initiative

Monique could choose to go about her business and complete her own part of the task. She could decide that she is not responsible for Brent's part of the work, that it is not her problem. But Monique makes another choice. She goes to her boss to explain the situation.

The boss checks the progress of the other teams and finds that he can move another person into the stockroom to work with Monique for an hour. He asks if Monique would be able to work overtime for an hour to get the job done. Monique says she can do this.

Before asking the boss to help her reschedule the workload, Monique was afraid that her part of the job would not be done on time because of Brent's absence. She is glad she went to the boss and found a way to handle the problem. The boss is very pleased with Monique's sense of responsibility. He sees that Monique is a good worker within a group.

The group effort at the sporting goods store was a success. Everything was ready for the sale.

Monique practiced self-management skills at work. She listened carefully to learn about the goal to be achieved. She made notes about the objectives she was to meet in her part of the job. She understood what the other employees were doing. She asked questions when she was uncertain about what to do.

In working with this group, Monique felt the effects of one group member not fulfilling his or her responsibilities. She saw how this could change the responsibilities and the schedules of others in the group. The members of the group needed each other, and they needed to work together.

Monique also found that by evaluating the progress and the problems in the situation, plans and schedules could be changed to meet a new need.

What if you're the one who's out sick? You can still practice self-management. Be sure to call in first thing in the morning or even the night before. When you get back to work, ask what you've missed. Or, better yet, take the extra time and effort to find out what needs to be caught up.

Monique's Accomplishments

The sale was a success; so was Monique. She had succeeded in doing her part in a group effort. She had understood the goal. She had learned which responsibilities were hers and which were the re-sponsibilities of others. She saw the importance of keeping on schedule. She showed initiative in evalu-ating the changing situation and seeing the need to restructure the plan. Monique had practiced self-management skills at work.

Questions to Ask Yourself

Self-management skills can help you accomplish goals at work. 1) Why is it important to understand exactly what is expected of you? 2) Have you ever been asked to do something only to find out that you don't have all of the information you need? Did you request more information? 3) In a group effort, why is it important to accomplish the part of the task that you are responsible for?

Self-Management in Activities

YOU HAVE SEEN HOW MICHAEL AND MONIQUE practiced self-management techniques and succeeded in meeting challenges. In both cases, someone helped them by outlining steps necessary to their success.

Michael's teacher gave him an outline to follow that told him what work was to be completed on what dates. Monique's boss at the store gave everyone tasks to accomplish to meet the deadline for the sale. Michael and Monique used self-management skills to increase their performance and reach their goals.

You can use the same effective skills to increase your performance and achieve goals that you set for yourself in your own activities. This idea presents yet another challenge. You will need to be responsible for the whole project.

Before you decide you don't want to take on anything harder than what you are trying to do now, read a bit further and see what may be in it for you.

The Need for Initiative

At school and at work, you usually have someone telling you what is expected of you. By seeing what must be accomplished, you can make plans for organizing your tasks and completing the project.

But what if there is something that you just want to do for yourself? No one has told you that it is something you must do. No one has ever said that if you do not do it, something bad will happen or you will miss out on something. What if there is something that you just want to do? If you want to do it, you need to take initiative. You need to be ready and able to take the first step on your own.

The same self-management skills used to succeed at school and on the job can be used to achieve your personal goal. You can increase your performance in the activity that you choose. You can go all out on your personal activity and do it better than you thought possible by managing yourself with the same effort that Michael and Monique used at school and on the job. The difference is that you will be doing it on your own and for yourself.

To Dream or to Act

There is a popular expression used to encourage people to accomplish things that they want to accomplish: "Go for it."

This is a great directive. But how do you "go for

it"? The people who tell you this don't always stick around and explain just how to go about "going for it." So you may end up just where you were before, dreaming about accomplishment. You do have another choice. You really can "go for it."

If there is something you really want to accomplish, you need to approach it as seriously as Michael approached his schoolwork. You need to follow those same steps.

Choosing Your Own Goal

Your first step in achieving high performance in your activity is to decide what you want to accomplish. Maybe you enjoy music and want to learn to play the piano. You may want to be able to play tennis. You can sit back and daydream about doing these things, or you can take action.

Maybe you can list lots of reasons why you cannot do the thing that you want to do. You may say that you *would* try that special activity but—and you can fill in all the things that stand in your way.

This is where your challenge comes in. Can you set a goal for yourself?

The Challenge of Independence

When a teacher or a boss or a parent tells you what to do, you can grumble about how you don't want to do it or what a bad idea it is. But the fact is that

Rather than dreaming about something you'd like to do, go ahead and try it.

you do not need to take responsibility for choosing the goal. It is all set out for you.

Sometimes it is easier to dream than to take initiative. Making an independent decision can be risky. You may fear failure. You may be afraid that someone will think poorly of you for trying to achieve your goals. It may just seem too hard.

On the other hand, if you are willing to take the risks, if you are willing to be independent and responsible for your choices and actions, *you may win.*

Planning Your Schedule

OK, so you are willing to act independently. What next? To succeed in your personal activity, you need to follow the same orderly steps that Michael and Monique did.

You need to break your goal down into smaller parts. You need to set up a schedule. If you have chosen to be a tennis player, your first step is not to sign up for a tennis tournament at school. First, you need to learn how to play the game. Be realistic in scheduling the steps you will take toward succeeding in your activity. You need to start at the beginning.

If you are serious about high performance in your activity, use a calendar to help you as you plan. Write down what you want to achieve and when you hope to achieve it. You may need to revise this later, but it will be a starting point.

Evaluating Your Progress

Since you are responsible for this plan, you need to set up a way to evaluate your progress. The evaluation process gives you a chance to change things on your schedule. You may find that you accomplish some steps in less time than you had expected. Other steps may take a bit longer. You may also find that you need to add some steps that you didn't even know about when you started.

The following is an example of a young man applying self-management skills to a personal activity of his choice.

Having a Dream

Antonio is in the tenth grade. He started attending school in a new neighborhood when his family moved. Antonio likes his new home and his new school, and he has made some new friends.

For many years Antonio had dreamed about playing on his high school basketball team. He had always played well in middle school, and he spent lots of time after school playing with the other kids in the neighborhood.

Now, Antonio found himself in a school with lots of people he didn't know. He didn't know the other guys on the basketball team. He didn't know the coach. He didn't know any of the plays that the team used. He felt his dream fading away. He couldn't see how he could accomplish it with so many obstacles.

Making Excuses

When Antonio's mother asked if he planned to try out for the team, Antonio said he would like to, but he didn't think he would have time because of homework. Later when his father asked if he had tried out for the team, Antonio said he would have but the team was already chosen for the year.

One day after school, Antonio was watching a talk show on television. A man on the show was explaining how some people make excuses not to do things that they want to do because they are afraid they might fail. So, rather than try, they blame other people and other things for not doing what they really want to do.

Antonio realized that this was exactly what he was doing. He was making excuses. He wanted to play on the basketball team but he was afraid to try.

Go for It

That day, he decided he would try out for the team. He set a realistic goal for himself. Since the basketball season was already under way, he would get ready to try out for next year's team. He would begin today!

Independent Scheduling

Antonio made a list of things he would need to do in order to be ready for tryouts.

1. Practice shooting baskets.
2. Watch the team practice and see how they play.
3. Go to all team games.

On his bedroom calendar he noted the dates of games and the days when the team practiced. Then he checked his schedule to see when he could shoot baskets at the court near his home. Antonio was choosing the objectives he would need to meet to help him achieve his goal.

Self-Evaluation

When Antonio started his project, he felt both scared and excited. As the days and weeks went by, he began to feel a little bored and discouraged. Could he really do this, or was he just wasting his time watching a bunch of people do what he wanted to be doing?

Antonio reread the list he had pinned on his bulletin board when he decided on his goal. He had been shooting baskets and keeping in shape. He had gone to all the home games and watched carefully how the guys interacted on the court.

He realized that he had left out an important step toward his goal. If he was to have a chance to try out for the team, he needed to meet the coach. This was just too hard for him. He was too shy to walk up to a man he didn't know and say, "Hi, I'm Antonio, I play basketball and hope to try out for next year's team." The coach might just ignore him or, worse yet, laugh at him. Antonio was saying to himself, "Well, I would like to meet the coach, but . . ."

Go for It Again

A new step would be added to the plan, Antonio decided. Not only would he meet the coach, but he would tell the coach that he wanted to try out for the team the following year and was watching practices to learn how the team played. He would risk it. He would take the initiative.

The next day at practice, Antonio spoke to the coach. Rather than laughing at him, the coach smiled and said he was glad that Antonio was interested in the team. He asked where Antonio had played before and said he would like to see him play during practice the following week.

Take a Bow

Antonio was on his way to accomplishing his personal activity goal. It had not been easy. He faced some difficult challenges. Antonio had to choose to act independently. He had to set his own goal and break it down into steps, or objectives. No one did this for him. He was on his own.

When it was time to evaluate his progress, he found that he needed to overcome his fears and take some bold steps. Antonio practiced self-management skills and learned that he was capable of doing things that he wanted to do for himself.

Questions to Ask Yourself

Initiative is your own willingness and ability to initiate, or start something. 1) Why is it important to have initiative? 2) What are some of the things that stop people from taking the initiative to start something? 3) Have you ever wanted to start something but didn't because you were afraid you would fail?

Self-Management for Future Success

YOU CAN SEE NOW THAT YOU CAN USE THE SAME principles of self-management to achieve high performance at school, at your job, and in your own personal activities. Besides using these tools to help you accomplish things you want now, you can use them to help you get the things you want for your future.

Maybe you haven't given any thought to what you want for your future. Maybe you have thought about it a lot and still have no idea what you want. Maybe you know exactly what you want but don't think you have a chance in the world of achieving it.

Whether you are prepared for it or not, it is probably a good idea to begin giving some thought to what you want for your future. If you have a pretty good idea already, then start your planning now.

There Is No Time Like the Present
You may have two more years of high school, but

that isn't too soon to start deciding where you are going when you leave school. Keep in mind that you do have a choice. How you end up spending your future depends partly on how you choose to spend it. You will arrive at your future through a series of days just like today. So what are you doing today that will help you get what you want? Once again, you need to consider that challenging word, "responsibility."

"I Would Have, But . . ."

Ten years from now, if you are doing a job you don't want to be doing, what reason will you give? You could even make a game of this with friends. Sit in a circle. First go around the circle and have each person say what work he or she wants to be doing in ten years. Then go around the circle and have everyone explain why they think they will or will not be doing that work. How many people use the phrase, "I would do this or that, but . . ."?

Frequently, people say that they would really like to be doing one thing but they are doing something else instead. Perhaps this is because the "something else" is easier to do. Or it may just be that they never sat down and thought about how they could be doing what they really want to do. Maybe they have never taken the responsibility to plan a course of action.

Your Future Starts Today

Planning your future can be a pretty big task. Up to this point, most decisions have been made for you. If you have not been taught self-management skills and had the opportunity to practice them, you may have no idea how to go about planning your future.

But that won't happen to you because you do know about self-management skills. You know about taking initiative and being responsible. You know about choosing goals and breaking them down into smaller parts. You know about scheduling your time, using a calendar, keeping track of your plans. You know how to evaluate your progress and revise your plan if needed. So, you are able to set your course for the future and begin the journey today.

Start at the Beginning

To begin planning for your future, think about what you would like to do. Choose something you enjoy doing or think you would enjoy doing. You will probably be most successful doing something you want to do because you will put more effort into it. Today's employer is looking for someone who is interested in the job and willing to learn more about it.

Once you have chosen the kind of work you want to do, you are ready for the second part of the goal-

It's never too early to start planning for the future.

setting process. What time frame do you wish to set for yourself? Be realistic. You may need to change this time frame later, but you need a starting point.

Now you should be able to state your long-term goal: In_____years, I will be_____. You know the next step. You break this big goal down into smaller parts that you can work on one by one. Make a list of all the steps you can think of that you will need to take to reach that goal.

You Have Lots of Choices
You may find at this point that you really have no

idea what you need to do to achieve this goal. So you have two choices: You can put the list down and forget about it, or you can go to the library and do some research on your career choice.

If you have decided to learn more about the steps needed to reach your goal, you have already made progress. Congratulations.

Your list may include going to some kind of trade school or college. It may include getting experience through part-time or volunteer work. It may include earning money to pay for the courses you will need. You can also learn about opportunities for financial aid.

As you proceed with your planning and scheduling, your list may continue to grow. Some items may at first seem too difficult to achieve. But as you meet your objectives and work toward the goal, those things may not seem so difficult anymore. You can probably do things now that you couldn't do a few years ago. You will continue to learn.

Blending the Present and the Future

Scheduling time for your future plan can be a little tricky. You are already busy trying to keep up with all the things you are supposed to be doing now. You have schoolwork, school activities, home chores, a job after school, or any number of other things you are trying to juggle and to remember!

You may find it is enough of a challenge to keep your schedule straight for next Tuesday, much less what you need to do next year. It may be a little easier to keep your future goal in mind if you can make it part of your present plans.

So how does one do that, you may wonder. There are different ways to accomplish it. If your goal is to be a writer, you might plan to take an extra English class. You might think about being a writer as you read your school assignments. You might apply to work for the school newspaper or look for a part-time job at a local newspaper.

If you want to be serious about your future, you will find ways to use the present to help you prepare.

Let's take a look at Heather as she begins to use today to plan for tomorrow.

Looking to the Future

Heather started to think about what she wanted to do after high school when she attended a career development class at school. She was dismayed because she had no idea in what direction she wanted to go.

The school counselor had suggested that Heather think about something she enjoyed doing at school and then consider how she could use that in a job. Heather knew she had always enjoyed art classes.

Volunteering can be a great way to gain experience in the field you're interested in.

She liked to draw, paint, and make hand-crafted items. But she didn't see how she could use that interest in any kind of work. She didn't know if there were jobs requiring her skills and interest in arts and crafts.

Then one day she visited her grandmother in a nursing home. Her grandmother showed her the art projects she had worked on that week in the activity group. Heather realized that there was a job at the nursing home for someone who taught arts and crafts. She began to think that this might be something she would enjoy doing some day. The more

Heather thought about it, the more she thought that she would like to learn more about the possibility.

Taking Advantage of Opportunity

In Heather's school, each student had the opportunity to do community service for school credit. She decided to choose the nursing home as a place to do volunteer work. In that way she could find out if she might be interested in working with senior citizens. Heather volunteered to assist the activity director on Sunday afternoons.

Using What You Learn at School

At school, Heather also signed up for another art class. This would help her gain more ideas and more skills to use in her volunteer work. She told her art teacher about the nursing home project, and the teacher offered to help Heather learn new skills for her work.

Heather made another appointment to talk with her counselor and told her about the nursing home work. The counselor gave Heather information on community college courses in working with older people and in teaching leisure skills. Heather had had no idea that such courses were available.

Taking these courses would cost money, but Heather was interested in finding out about them.

She already had a part-time job. She decided that if she began saving some of her money she would be able to go to community college. She also learned that some financial aid was available. She decided that if she liked the nursing home work, she might try to go to college after high school.

Getting Work Experience

By volunteering in the nursing home, Heather was getting experience in working with other people and taking responsibility on the job. Employers are interested in hiring people who already know how to handle themselves in the workplace. On the job, a person must be able to interact with other people.

Heather took the opportunity to see if she could work with other staff members, follow the directions of a supervisor, and interact with the residents of the nursing home. This offered her a chance to learn about her own work skills and to watch others who were already in the workforce.

By doing the volunteer work, Heather was earning the school credit she needed. By taking an extra art class, she was doing something she enjoyed. But Heather was also doing something to plan for her future. She had considered her future when she made her choices.

Heather used her self-management skills to make good use of her time. She set a goal of learning about employment possibilities using her interest in arts and crafts. She took the initiative to find a place to try out her skills. Then she scheduled her time to allow herself to follow through on her plans.

Self-management was helping Heather prepare for a productive future. This would be a future that didn't just happen, but one that she shaped by her actions and choices.

Questions to Ask Yourself

One of the major challenges of becoming an adult is learning to make your own decisions about the future. 1) What kind of work might you like to do in the future? 2) If you are not certain what steps you need to take to achieve that career goal, how can you find out? 3) If you are not yet certain what kind of work you would like to do, like Heather, where is a good place to start?

Conclusion:
The Beginning

YOU KNOW NOW WHAT SELF-MANAGEMENT IS.
You know that this group of skills can help you be
more successful in what you are doing today and
what you will be doing tomorrow.

These skills are tools that you can put to use in
your life. Like Michael, you may need to improve
your schoolwork by taking responsibility for your
assignments.

At your part-time job, you may want to show
your boss that you are a good employee and that
you deserve a raise. You can use your self-management skills to work better within your group. You
can show the boss that you know how to take initiative. You can take action without being prompted.

You will also find ways to perform better in your
leisure activities and hobbies. You can do this because you know more about working independently
and scheduling your time.

That future of yours that seems so far away is
right around the corner. You know that you can use

your new self-management skills to help you get some of the things you want for your future. You can plan and use your time wisely now.

But while you are doing something good for yourself, your future employer will also see that you have done something very good for your career. The skills you have read about and seen demonstrated by Michael, Monique, Antonio, and Heather are skills that will make you stand out in the workplace.

Self-management skills will help you to perform a job in an organized manner because you will know how to plan and schedule your time and evaluate your progress.

Self-management skills will give you the kind of initiative and sense of responsibility that will make a boss confident in you. You will be able to show the boss that you can be relied on to act independently when necessary. In the busy workplaces of today, employers want to know that workers can perform their jobs without constant supervision and reminders.

Self-management skills will help you face a large project or handle a complicated problem. You will have the skill to break the project down into smaller parts. You will be able to set the goal and schedule the steps along the way. An employer will see that you can handle more difficult tasks because you know how to approach them. This is the kind of skill that can result in promotion.

It can be worth your time to begin applying your new self-management skills today. Think about how you could schedule your time better for your schoolwork. Ask yourself if you are showing responsibility at your job. What about your future? Have you made any plans yet?

As you practice your new skills, you will begin to improve your performance. You will find that you can achieve *high performance through self-management.*

Questions to Ask Yourself

Many skills that we learn are useful only at school or only at work. 1) How can self-management skills help you at school? 2) How can self-management skills help you at work? 3) Why is it important to plan for the future today?

Glossary

accomplish To succeed; to reach a goal.

challenge To confront or defy.

cooperation The process of acting with others.

directive A specific order or instruction to perform an action.

evaluate To judge the effectiveness of something.

excuse Explanation for failure to complete an obligation.

goal Something one strives to attain or achieve.

independence Ability to act for oneself, without control or influence by another.

initiative The ability to take the first step.

leisure Time free from work or duty (ease).

objective Something one aims at; a step toward a larger goal.

responsibility State of being accountable for an action; reliable, trustworthy.

schedule (noun) Plan of action in a specified time sequence; (verb) to plan one's work or actions with reference to time.

self-evaluation Process of rating or appraising one's efforts or achievements.

self-management The organized directing of one's own activities.

time frame The period of time during which something takes place.

volunteer work The practice of giving one's time and effort without payment, as for charity.

For Further Reading

Baumeister, Roy F. *Losing Control: How and Why People Fail at Self-Regulation*. San Diego: Academic Press, 1994.

Blanchard, Kenneth, and Johnson, Spencer. *The One Minute Manager*. New York: The Berkley Publishing Group, 1983.

Brewner, M. *Job Survival Skills*. New York: Educational Design, 1988.

Carnevale, Anthony P.; Gainer, Leila J.; and Meltzer, Ann S. *Workplace Basics: The Skills Employers Want*. San Francisco: Jossey-Bass, 1990.

Dahl, Dan, and Sykes, Randolph. *Charting Your Goals*. New York: Harper & Row, 1988.

Dayhoff, Signe A. *Get the Job You Want: Successful Strategies for Selling Yourself in the Job Market*. Acton, MA: Brick House Publishing Co., 1990.

DeVenzio, Dick. *Smart Moves, How to Succeed In School, Sports, Career, and Life*. Buffalo, New York: Prometheus Books, 1989.

Gilbert, Sara D. *Go for It: Get Organized*. New York: Morrow Junior Books, 1990.

Johnson, Linda Carlson. *Responsibility*. New York: The Rosen Publishing Group, 1990.

Lakein, Alan. *How to Get Control of Your Time and Your Life*. New York: P.H. Wyden, 1973.

McFarland, Rhoda. *The World of Work*. New York: The Rosen Publishing Group, 1993.

Smith, Sandra Lee. *Setting Goals*. New York: The Rosen Publishing Group, 1992.

Wirths, Claudine G., and Bowman-Kruhm, Mary. *Where's My Other Sock? How to Get Organized and Drive Your Parents and Teachers Crazy*. New York: Thomas Y. Crowell, 1989.

Index

About the Author
Peggy Santamaria has worked as a journalist and photographer, and has taught at the elementary and junior high school levels. She currently works in the field of banking and lives with her husband and daughters in Maryland.

Photos
Katherine Hsu

Layout and Design
Kim Sonsky

Acknowledgments
Thank you to Aimee Thomas for her assistance in preparing this text.